Jane Eyre

Someone was in my room. It was a woman. She was a big woman, tall and strong. At first I did not see her face. She looked at herself in the mirror. Then I saw her face! It was the most terrible face! She looked angry, cruel and frightening.

Jane Eyre works for Mr Rochester. At his large house, Thornfield Hall, she teaches the little girl, Adèle. But she also loves Mr Rochester, and wants to marry him. Does Rochester love her? Is Jane right to love him?

Rochester is very rich, and Jane is poor. But more important than that – there is a secret in Thornfield Hall, a terrible secret. Only Rochester knows what it is – and he will say nothing . . .

Charlotte Brontë was born in 1816 in a village in Yorkshire, England. After her mother died, in 1821, an aunt looked after Charlotte, her four sisters and their brother, Branwell. In 1824 the four oldest sisters, Maria, Elizabeth, Charlotte and Emily, went away to school. The school was a cold, terrible place, and because of it Maria and Elizabeth were ill and died. It is this school that Charlotte later described as 'Lowood' in *Jane Eyre*. After that Charlotte and her two sisters and Branwell had their lessons at home and they began to write stories together. She later worked as a teacher and then, for two years, she studied German and French in Brussels.

In 1844, Charlotte returned home and she and her sisters all began writing books. Emily wrote *Wuthering Heights* and Anne wrote *Agnes Grey*, and both sold their books – they came out together at the end of 1847. Charlotte could not sell her book, *The Professor*, but she tried again – and wrote *Jane Eyre*. This also came out in 1847 and readers loved it.

Charlotte was now famous, but terrible unhappiness followed. Her brother and sisters all died: Branwell in September 1848, Emily in December of that year, and Anne in 1849. Charlotte wrote two more books, *Shirley* in 1849 and *Villette* in 1853. She

The following titles are available at Levels 2, 3 and 4:

Level 2
Baywatch
The Birds
The Canterville Ghost and the Model
  Millionaire
The Cay
Chocky
The Diary
Don't Look Behind You
Don't Look Now
Emily
Flour Babies
The Fox
Free Willy
The Ghost of Genny Castle
Grandad's Eleven
Jumanji
The Lady in the Lake
Little Women
Money to Burn
Persuasion
The Railway Children
The Room in the Tower and Other
  Ghost Stories
The Secret Garden
The Sheep-Pig
Simply Suspense
Slinky Jane
Stealing the Hills
Treasure Island
The Treasure Seekers
Under the Greenwood Tree
The Wave
We Are All Guilty
The Weirdo

Level 3
Black Beauty
The Black Cat and Other Stories
The Book of Heroic Failures
Braveheart
Calling All Monsters
A Catskill Eagle
Channel Runner
Cranford
The Darling Buds of May
Dubliners
Earthdark
Eraser
Forrest Gump
The Fugitive
Get Shorty

Goggle Eyes
King Solomon's Mines
Madame Doubtfire
The Man with Two Shadows and Other
  Ghost Stories
More Heroic Failures
Mrs Dalloway
My Fair Lady
My Family and Other Animals
Not a Penny More, Not a Penny Less
NYPD Blue: Blue Beginning
The Portrait of a Lady
Rain Man
The Reluctant Queen
Santorini
Sense and Sensibility
Sherlock Holmes and the Mystery of
  Boscombe Pool
St Agnes' Stand
StarGate
Summer of My German Soldier
The Thirty-nine Steps
Thunder Point
Time Bird
The Turn of the Screw
Twice Shy

Level 4
The Boys from Brazil
The Breathing Method
The Burden of Proof
The Client
The Danger
Detective Work
The Doll's House and Other Stories
Dracula
Far from the Madding Crowd
Farewell, My Lovely
Glitz
Gone with the Wind, Part 1
Gone with the Wind, Part 2
The House of Stairs
The Locked Room and Other Horror
  Stories
The Lost World
The Mill on the Floss
The Mosquito Coast
The Picture of Dorian Gray
Seven
Strangers on a Train
White Fang

For a complete list of the titles available in the Penguin Readers series please write to
the following address for a catalogue: Penguin ELT Marketing Department, Penguin
Books Ltd, 27 Wrights Lane, London W8 5TZ.

Jane Eyre

CHARLOTTE BRONTË

Level 3

Retold by Ann Ward
Series Editor: Derek Strange

PENGUIN BOOKS

PENGUIN BOOKS

Published by the Penguin Group
Penguin Books Ltd, 27 Wrights Lane, London W8 5TZ, England
Penguin Books USA Inc., 375 Hudson Street, New York, New York 10014, USA
Penguin Books Australia Ltd, Ringwood, Victoria, Australia
Penguin Books Canada Ltd, 10 Alcorn Avenue, Toronto, Ontario, Canada M4V 3B2
Penguin Books (NZ) Ltd, 182–190 Wairau Road, Auckland 10, New Zealand

Penguin Books Ltd, Registered Offices: Harmondsworth, Middlesex, England

Jane Eyre was first published in 1847
This adaptation published by Penguin Books 1991
7 9 10 8 6

Text copyright © Ann Ward 1991
Illustrations copyright © Richard Johnson 1991
All rights reserved

The moral right of the adapter and of the illustrator has been asserted

Illustrations by Richard Johnson
Designed by D W Design Partnership Ltd

Printed in England by Clays Ltd, St Ives plc
Set in 11/14pt Lasercomp Bembo

To the teacher:

In addition to all the language forms of Levels One and Two, which are used again at this level of the series, the main verb forms and tenses used at Level Three are:

- past continuous verbs, present perfect simple verbs, conditional clauses (using the 'first' or 'open future' conditional), question tags and further common phrasal verbs
- modal verbs: *have* (*got*) *to* and *don't have to* (to express obligation), *need to* and *needn't* (to express necessity), *could* and *was able to* (to describe past ability), *could* and *would* (in offers and polite requests for help), and *shall* (future plans, offers and suggestions).

Also used are:

- relative pronouns: *who*, *that* and *which* (in defining clauses)
- conjunctions: *if* and *since* (for time or reason), *so that* (for purpose or result) and *while*
- indirect speech (questions)
- participle clauses.

Specific attention is paid to vocabulary development in the Vocabulary Work exercises at the end of the book. These exercises are aimed at training students to enlarge their vocabulary systematically through intelligent reading and effective use of a dictionary.

To the student:

Dictionary Words:

- As you read this book, you will find that some words are darker black than the others on the page. Look them up in your dictionary, if you do not already know them, or try to guess the meaning of the words first, without a dictionary.

John picked up a large, heavy book and threw it straight at me.

Jane Eyre

My name is Jane Eyre and my story begins when I was ten. I was living with my aunt, Mrs Reed, because my mother and father were both dead. Mrs Reed was rich. Her house was large and beautiful, but I was not happy there. Mrs Reed had three children, Eliza, John and Georgiana. My cousins were older than I. They never wanted to play with me and they were often unkind. I was afraid of them.

I was most afraid of my cousin John. He enjoyed frightening me and making me feel unhappy. One afternoon, I hid from him in a small room. I had a book with a lot of pictures in it and I felt quite happy. John and his sisters were with their mother.

But then John decided to look for me.

'Where's Jane Eyre?' he shouted, 'Jane! Jane! Come out!' He could not find me at first – he was not quick or clever. But then Eliza, who was clever, found my hiding place.

'Here she is!' she shouted. I had to come out. And John was waiting for me.

'What do you want?' I asked him.

'I want you to come here,' John said. I went and stood in front of him. He looked at me for a long time, and then suddenly he hit me. 'Now go and stand near the door!' he said.

I was very frightened. I knew that John wanted to hurt me. I went and stood near the door. Then John picked up a large, heavy book and threw it straight at me. The book hit me on the head and I fell.

'You **cruel** boy!' I shouted. 'You always want to hurt me. Look!' I touched my head. There was blood on it.

John **became** angrier. He ran across the room and started to hit me again and again. I was hurt and afraid, so I hit him back.

When at last I woke up, I was in my bed. The doctor was there. 'What happened?' I asked him.

Mrs Reed heard the noise and hurried into the room. She was very angry. She did not seem to notice the blood on my head.

'Jane Eyre! You bad girl!' she shouted. 'Why are you hitting your poor cousin? Take her away! Take her to the red room and lock the door!'

The red room was cold and dark. I was very frightened. Nobody ever went into the red room at night. I cried for help, but nobody came. 'Please help me!' I called, 'Don't leave me here!'

But nobody came to open the door. I cried for a long time, and then everything suddenly went black. I remember nothing after that.

When at last I woke up, I was in my bed. My head was hurting. The doctor was there. 'What happened?' I asked him.

'You are ill, Jane,' the doctor answered. 'Tell me, Jane. Are you unhappy here with your aunt and your cousins?'

'Yes, I am,' I answered. 'I'm very unhappy.'

'I see,' said the doctor. 'Would you like to go away to school?' he asked.

'Oh, yes, I think so,' I told him. The doctor looked at me again, and then he left the room. He talked to Mrs Reed for a long time. They decided to send me away to school.

So not long afterwards, I left my aunt's house to go to school. Mrs Reed and my cousins were pleased when I went away. I was not really sad to leave. 'Perhaps I'll be happy at school,' I thought. 'Perhaps I'll have some friends there.'

◆   ◆   ◆   ◆

One night in January, after a long journey, I arrived at Lowood School. It was dark and the weather was cold, windy and rainy.

The school was very large, but it was not warm and comfortable, like Mrs Reed's house. A teacher took me into a big room. It was full of girls. There were about eighty girls there. The youngest girls were nine, and the eldest were about twenty. They all wore ugly brown dresses.

It was supper time. There was water to drink, and a small piece of bread to eat. I was thirsty, and drank some water. I could not eat anything because I felt too tired and too excited. After supper, all the girls went upstairs to bed. The teacher took me into a very long room. All the girls slept in this room. Two girls had to sleep in each bed.

Early in the morning, I woke up. It was still dark outside and the room was very cold. The girls washed themselves in cold water and put on their brown dresses. Then everybody went downstairs and the early morning lessons began.

A teacher took me into a big room. It was full of girls. There were about eighty girls there.

At last, it was time for breakfast. I was now very hungry. We went into the dining-room with the teachers. There was a terrible smell of burning food. We were all hungry, but when we tasted the food we could not eat it. It tasted terrible. Feeling very hungry, we all left the dining-room.

At nine o'clock, lessons began again. I looked round at the other girls. They looked very strange in their ugly brown dresses. I did not like the teachers. They seemed to be unkind and unfriendly.

Then at twelve o'clock, the head teacher, Miss Temple, came in. She was very pretty and her face was kind. 'I want to speak to all the girls,' she said. 'I know that you could not eat your breakfast this morning,' she told us. 'So now you will have some bread and cheese and a cup of coffee.' The other teachers looked surprised. 'I'll pay for this meal,' Miss Temple said. The girls were very pleased.

After this meal, we went out into the garden. The girls' brown dresses were too thin for the cold winter weather. Most of the girls looked cold and unhappy, and some of them looked very ill. I walked around and looked at the girls and at the school and the garden. But I did not speak to anyone, and nobody spoke to me.

One of the girls was reading a book. 'Is your book interesting?' I asked her.

'I like it,' she answered.

'Does this school belong to Miss Temple?' I asked.

'No, it doesn't,' she answered. 'It belongs to Mr Brocklehurst. He buys all our food and all our clothes.'

The girl's name was Helen Burns. She was older than I was. I liked her immediately. She became my friend.

Helen told me that many of the girls were ill because they were always cold and hungry. Mr Brocklehurst was not a kind man. The clothes he bought for the girls were not warm enough for the winter, and there was never enough food to eat.

I went to Miss Temple's room. Helen Burns was lying there in a little bed. She was now very thin, and her face was white.

After a few months, many of the girls at Lowood School became seriously ill. Lessons stopped, and I and the other girls who were not ill spent all our time out in the fields near the school. The weather was now warm and sunny. It was a happy time for us, but my friend Helen Burns was not with us. She had to stay in bed. She was very ill.

One evening, I went to Miss Temple's room. Helen Burns was lying there in a little bed. She was now very thin, and her face was white. She spoke to me in a low voice. 'Jane,' she said, 'it's good to see you. I want to say goodbye to you.'

'Why?' I asked her. 'Are you going away?'

'Yes, I am,' Helen answered. 'I'm going far away.'

That night she died.

During that summer, many other girls in the school died too. Mr Brocklehurst sold the school, and it became a happier place.

I stayed at the school until I was eighteen and then I had to find a job. I wanted to become a teacher.

I wrote a letter to a newspaper. I said I was a young teacher, who wanted a job working in a family. Then I waited for an answer. At last, an answer came. It was from a **lady**, Mrs Fairfax, who lived at a place called Thornfield Hall. She needed a teacher for a little girl. So I **packed** my clothes in a small bag and travelled to Thornfield Hall.

♦   ♦   ♦   ♦

I felt very excited when I arrived at Thornfield Hall. The house was large, but it seemed very quiet. Mrs Fairfax met me at the door. She was an old lady with a kind face.

'Sit down, Miss Eyre,' she said. 'You look tired after your journey. Later, you will meet Adèle.'

'Is Adèle my student?' I asked.

'Yes, she is. She is French. Mr Rochester wants you to teach her English.'

'Who is Mr Rochester?' I asked.

Mrs Fairfax looked surprised. 'Did you not know? Thornfield Hall belongs to Mr Rochester,' she answered. 'I only work for him.'

'Is Mr Rochester here now?' I asked.

'No. He is away. He does not come very often to Thornfield. I do not know when he will return.'

Later, I met Adèle. She was a pretty little girl. I spoke to her in French, and began to teach her English. She enjoyed her lessons, and I enjoyed teaching her. I liked Adèle and I liked Mrs Fairfax, too. It was quiet at Thornfield Hall, and sometimes I felt a little bored, but everybody was kind to me there.

One afternoon, I walked to the village to post a letter. It was winter, and there was ice on the road. As I was walking back to Thornfield Hall, I heard a noise behind me. It was a horse. A man was riding towards Thornfield Hall. I stood on one side and the horse went past. The man did not see me. He was a stranger with dark hair. Suddenly, with a loud noise, the stranger's horse fell down on the ice. The man was lying on the ground, trying to get up. I ran forward to help.

'Are you hurt, sir?' I asked him.

The stranger looked surprised to see me. 'A little,' he answered. 'Could you help me to catch my horse? That's right. Now could you bring the horse here, please? Thank you.' The stranger tried to stand up, but his leg was hurting too much. He looked at me again. 'Could you help me to get up on its back again? Good. Thank you, Miss.'

I watched him as he rode away. 'Who is he?' I asked myself. 'He is not handsome, but he has an interesting face. I would like to know him.'

When I got back to Thornfield, everybody was very excited. Mrs Fairfax was very busy. 'What's happening?' I asked her.

'Oh, Miss Eyre,' said Mrs Fairfax, 'it is Mr Rochester! He has suddenly come back! But he will probably go away again soon. Now, Miss Eyre, you must go and put on your best dress. Mr Rochester wants to meet you and Adèle after dinner.'

Later that evening, I took Adèle to Mr Rochester's room. I felt rather afraid of meeting Mr Rochester. I went quietly into the room and saw a man there. I knew him. It was the man on the horse. So the interesting stranger was Mr Rochester!

Mr Rochester did not go away again. He was busy every day but sometimes in the evenings he talked to me. He was usually serious, and he did not smile or laugh very often, but

A man was riding towards Thornfield Hall. Suddenly, with a loud noise, the stranger's horse fell down on the ice.

Mr Rochester was asleep and the bed was on fire! Quickly, I took some water and threw it all over the bed.

he was interesting and I was not afraid of him. I began to enjoy myself more at Thornfield Hall.

♦   ♦   ♦   ♦

One night, I woke up suddenly. It was about two o'clock in the morning. I thought I heard a sound. Everything was very quiet. I listened carefully and the sound came again. Someone was walking about outside my room.

'Who's there?' I called. Nobody answered. I felt cold and frightened. The house was silent. I tried to sleep again.

Then I heard a laugh. It was a terrible, cruel laugh! I listened. Someone was walking away, going up the stairs to the **attic**. What was happening? I decided to go and find Mrs

Fairfax. I put on some clothes and left my room. The house was quiet now, but suddenly I could smell smoke. Something was burning! I ran to find out.

The smoke was coming from Mr Rochester's room. I ran into the room and looked around. Mr Rochester was asleep in his bed, and the bed was on fire! 'What can I do?' I thought. Quickly, I looked around the room. Luckily, there was some water in one corner. As quickly as I could, I took the water and threw it all over the bed. Mr Rochester woke up.

'What's happening?' he shouted. 'Jane! Is it you? What are you doing?'

'Mr Rochester,' I said, 'your bed is on fire! You must get up at once.'

He jumped out of bed. There was water everywhere and the fire was still smoking. 'Jane, you've saved me from the fire! How did you know about it? Why did you wake up?' Mr Rochester asked. I told him about the noise outside my door and the terrible laugh.

Mr Rochester looked serious and angry. 'I must go upstairs to the attic. Stay here and wait for me, please. Do not wake Mrs Fairfax.' He left the room and I waited for him.

At last, he came back. He was still looking very serious. 'You can go back to bed, now, Jane. Everything is all right now.'

'Who lives in the attic?' I asked Mrs Fairfax the next day.

'Only Grace Poole,' she answered. 'She is one of the **servants**. She is a strange woman.'

I remembered Grace Poole. She was a strange, silent woman, who did not often speak to the other servants. So perhaps it was Grace Poole who walked around the house late at night and laughed strangely outside the doors.

That evening, when Adèle finished her lessons, I went downstairs. Mrs Fairfax met me. 'Mr Rochester left the house early this morning,' she said. 'He is going to stay with his friends. I think he will stay with them for some weeks. I do not know when he will come back.'

For several weeks, the house was very quiet again. Mr Rochester stayed with his friends and I continued my lessons with Adèle. I did not hear the strange and terrible laugh at night again.

One day, Mrs Fairfax showed me a letter from Mr Rochester. 'He is coming back,' she said, 'and he is bringing a lot of visitors with him. I am going to be very busy getting everything ready. Miss Blanche Ingram is coming too. She is very beautiful.'

Mr Rochester and his friends arrived. The visitors were all rich, important people. Miss Blanche Ingram was among them. She was beautiful but very proud. Some of the visitors were nice to me, but the others did not notice me. I was too poor and unimportant. Miss Ingram never spoke to me. She was not interested in me, but she seemed to be interested in Mr Rochester. She always seemed to enjoy her conversations with him. They often went out riding together.

'I think Mr Rochester will marry Miss Ingram,' said Mrs Fairfax.

But was Mr Rochester interested in Blanche Ingram? He seemed to like her, but he did not look very happy when they were together.

◆   ◆   ◆   ◆

One evening, a new visitor came to Thornfield Hall. He was a quiet young man with dark hair called Mr Mason. He came to see Mr Rochester on business. Mr Mason told us that he and Mr Rochester were old friends, but Mr Rochester was not very pleased to see Mr Mason. When Mr Rochester heard the name 'Mr Mason, from the West Indies', he was surprised and his face turned white.

That night, Mr Rochester and Mr Mason talked for a long

Blanche Ingram seemed to be interested in Mr Rochester. They often went out riding together.

time. At last, very late at night, they went to bed. Soon, everyone in the house was asleep. Suddenly, I woke up. I heard a terrible scream from somewhere over my head. Then everything was very quiet again. I listened carefully, and then I heard a lot of noise from above my head. There seemed to be fighting in the room above. Then there was another scream.

'Help! Help!' someone shouted. There was more fighting. Then a voice called out 'Rochester! Come quickly! Help me!'

A door opened, and I heard someone running up the stairs to the attic. I quickly put on some clothes and opened my door. Everybody in the house was awake now. The visitors were all standing outside their doors.

'What's happening? Is there a fire? What was that noise?' they asked.

Mr Rochester came down from the attic. 'Please don't worry,' he told his friends. 'Everything is all right.'

'But what's happening?' somebody asked.

'One of the servants had a bad dream and started to scream,' Mr Rochester said. 'But everything is all right now. Please go back to bed.'

Slowly, all Mr Rochester's visitors returned to their rooms. I too went back to my room, but I did not go back to bed. I sat and looked out of the window. The house was very quiet now. There were no sounds from the attic.

Then someone knocked on my door. I opened it. Mr Rochester stood outside. 'Jane, come with me please,' he told me, 'but come quietly . . . follow me.'

I followed Mr Rochester up to the attic. He unlocked the door of a room and we went inside.

'Wait here,' Mr Rochester told me. I stood next to the door. There was another door on the opposite side of the room. From behind this door I could hear a terrible sound. It was like an angry animal. Mr Rochester left me and went through this door. Once again, I heard that terrible, cruel laugh! Was Grace Poole behind the door? Mr Rochester spoke to someone inside the room, and then came out and locked the door again.

'Come here, Jane,' he told me quietly. I came further into the room. There was a large bed in the room. Mr Mason was lying on the bed. His face was white and his eyes were closed. There was a lot of blood on his shirt. He did not move.

'Is he dead?' I asked.

'No,' answered Mr Rochester. 'He isn't badly hurt but I must go and bring the doctor for him. Will you stay with him until I get back?'

The man on the bed moved, and tried to speak. Mr Rochester turned to him. 'Don't try to talk, Mason. Jane, do not speak to him, please. There must be no conversation between you.'

Mr Rochester hurried out of the room. I waited for him with the silent man on the bed. I was frightened. I knew that Grace Poole was in the next room. For a long time, I waited for Mr Rochester to return. 'When will he come back?' I asked myself.

At last morning came and Mr Rochester returned with the doctor. While the doctor was looking after Mr Mason, Mr Rochester spoke to me. 'Thank you for all your help, Jane. Mason is going to leave Thornfield Hall now. The doctor will take him away,' he told me.

We helped Mr Mason down the stairs and out of the house. It was still early, and the other people in the house were still asleep.

'Take care of poor Mason,' said Mr Rochester to the doctor. 'Soon he will be able to go back home to the West Indies.'

Before he left, Mr Mason said something very strange. 'Look after her, Rochester,' he said. 'Promise to look after her.'

I waited for Mr Rochester's return with the silent man on the bed. I was
frightened, I knew that Grace Poole was in the next room.

Mr Rochester looked sad. 'I promise. I will always look after her.'

I started to go back to the house. 'Don't go, Jane,' said Mr Rochester. 'Come into the garden. Talk to me.'

We went into the garden. 'What a night!' he said. 'Were you frightened, Jane?'

'Yes, I was frightened. Up there, in the next room . . . there was someone . . . that terrible laugh . . . Mr Rochester, will Grace Poole go away now?'

'No,' he replied. 'But don't worry about Grace Poole. Try to forget about her. She isn't dangerous. It is Mason I am worrying about.'

I was surprised to hear this. 'Mr Mason? But he is frightened. He can't hurt you.'

Mr Rochester looked sad. 'I know Mason does not want to hurt me, but he could say something that will hurt me. I shall be happier when he goes back to the West Indies.'

♦   ♦   ♦   ♦

Later that day, I got a surprising letter. Mrs Reed, my aunt, was dying and she wanted to see me. It was a long journey to her home. When I got there, I heard that my cousin John was dead. Mrs Reed was very ill. At first, she did not want to speak to me. Then one day, when I was sitting by her bed, she showed me a letter. It was from my uncle, my father's brother, who lived in Madeira. This was the letter:

Dear Mrs Reed,
Please help me. I want to find my brother's daughter, Jane Eyre. I am a rich man and I have no children. I want Jane Eyre to come and live with me.

Yours sincerely,
John Eyre.

I read the letter and looked at the date on it. 'But, Mrs Reed,' I said, 'this is an old letter. You got it three years ago!'

'I know,' she said, 'but I never liked you, Jane Eyre. After I read the letter, I wrote to your uncle. I told him you were dead. I told him you died at Lowood School. Now go away! Leave me!'

Soon afterwards, Mrs Reed died, and I returned to Thornfield Hall. It was summer, and the fields around Thornfield Hall were very quiet and beautiful. For me, it was the most beautiful place in the world. It was my home now.

'Adèle will be pleased to see me,' I thought. 'But what about Mr Rochester? He is the person I most want to see. But does he want to see me? Perhaps by now he is already married to Blanche Ingram. If they are not already married, they will be married very soon.' I felt sad when I thought about Mr Rochester and Blanche Ingram. 'So I must soon leave this beautiful place,' I thought. 'I can't stay here when Mr Rochester is married. I will never see Thornfield Hall again. And worse than that, I will never see Mr Rochester again.'

As I came near the house, I met Mr Rochester. When I saw that he looked pleased to see me, I felt happier. Adèle and Mrs Fairfax were happy to see me too. 'The visitors have all left now,' said Mrs Fairfax. 'It is very quiet here. It is good to see you again.'

'Yes, this is my home,' I thought. 'I've always been happy here. How can I leave it?'

I started to work, teaching Adèle again. Everything was the same as before. Mr Rochester still said nothing about getting married to Blanche Ingram. Then one evening, he saw me in the garden. 'Come and talk to me, Jane,' he said.

I went towards him. 'Now,' I thought, 'he's going to tell me that he is going to get married.'

'Are you happy here, Jane?' he asked.

'Yes, I am, very happy,' I answered.

'And you like Adèle and Mrs Fairfax?'

'Very much,' I said.

'You'll be sad to leave them,' he said.

I looked away. 'Now he is going to tell me that I must leave because he is going to be married,' I thought. I looked at him. 'Yes,' I answered, 'I will be very sad to leave.'

'But you must leave, you know,' Mr Rochester said.

'Must I? Must I leave soon?'

'Yes, soon.'

'Then you are going to get married.'

'Yes, I am going to get married. Adèle must go to school, and you must get a new job. I will find you one. Far from here.'

'Far from here?' I asked. 'But then I'll never see Thornfield Hall again, and . . . and I'll never see you again, Mr Rochester.'

'Oh, when you are far from here, you'll soon forget me,' he said.

'No,' I thought, 'you will forget me perhaps, but I will never forget you.'

'Never,' I answered him, at last. And I started to cry. I could not speak.

He watched me carefully, then at last he spoke again. 'Perhaps you do not need to go,' he said. 'Perhaps you can stay here when I am married?'

Did Mr Rochester think that I had no feelings? Did he not understand how I felt? Were my feelings so unimportant? I now felt angry.

'No,' I told him. 'I could never stay. I will not stay. Miss Ingram . . . Miss Ingram will be your wife. I know that I am not rich and beautiful like Miss Ingram. I am poor and

Mr Rochester wanted to marry me! He wanted me to be his wife!

unimportant. But I can still feel sadness. And if you marry Miss Ingram, I must leave here.'

Mr Rochester looked at me, and then he smiled. 'I don't want you to go, Jane. And I am not going to marry Miss Ingram. Don't get excited. I want you to stay here. It's you I want to marry.'

I could not believe him. 'Now you are laughing at me,' I said.

'No, I am not,' he answered. 'I want you to marry me, Jane. Will you marry me?'

He looked at me so seriously that at last I did believe him. Mr Rochester wanted to marry me! He wanted me to be his wife!

'Yes, I will marry you,' I answered.

'I will make you happy, Jane,' he said. 'No one will stop us,' he continued, with a strange, half-sad look. I could not understand that look, but I was too happy to be worried about it.

It grew dark. The wind began to blow, and it started to rain, so we walked together back to the house.

♦ ♦ ♦ ♦

My wedding day was only a month later. Two nights before the wedding, I was in bed, asleep. My wedding dress was in the room. It was a windy night. The wind made a strange sound. Suddenly, I woke up. There was a light in the room. I thought it was morning, but it was still dark outside.

Someone was in my room. Was it Mrs Fairfax? Was it Grace Poole? It was neither of them. It was a woman, but I did not know her. She was a big woman, tall and strong. Her black hair was long and thick. Her clothes were long and white. At first I did not see her face. She took my dress and held it in front of her. She looked at herself in the mirror. Then I saw her face!

It was the most terrible face! The woman's eyes were large and red and her face was purple. She looked angry, cruel and frightening.

Then she took my dress, and angrily **tore** it to pieces. She threw the pieces of the dress on the floor. Next, she went to the window, and looked out. Then she started to come towards my bed. I was so frightened that I could not move. I could not scream for help. I lay still in bed. 'Is she going to kill me?' I thought. But suddenly the light disappeared and the room went dark.

When I woke up, it was morning. The sun was shining. At once, I remembered that strange and frightening woman. Did it all really happen or was it a **dream**? Did she really come into my room in the middle of the night? Then I saw my

'Jane, I think you had a bad dream, I think it was perhaps Grace Poole who really tore your dress.

wedding dress. It was lying on the floor, **torn** to pieces, I picked up the pieces of the dress. So it was all true! That terrible woman was real!

When I told Mr Rochester about the woman and showed him my dress, he looked very worried and was silent for a long time.

'Jane, I think you had a bad dream,' he said at last. 'I think it was perhaps Grace Poole who really tore your dress, but in your dream it was some stranger.'

I was not sure about this, but I said nothing. That night, the night before the wedding, I slept in Adèle's room.

My wedding day came, and we went to the church. But

the wedding did not happen. In the church, while the clergyman was speaking, someone threw open the doors at the back and shouted 'Stop the wedding! Mr Rochester cannot get married! He has got a wife already! He is married to my sister!'

Everybody in the church turned round to see the speaker. It was Mr Mason, the man from the West Indies. But who was his sister? How could Mr Rochester be married? I could not believe it. My heart turned to ice. I looked at Mr Rochester. His face was white and hard. But he did not say that Mr Mason was mistaken.

'But where is Mr Rochester's wife, your sister?' the clergyman asked Mr Mason. 'Where does she live?'

'She lives at Thornfield Hall,' answered Mr Mason. 'She is still alive. I saw her there last April.'

'At Thornfield Hall!' the clergyman said. 'But I know of no Mrs Rochester at Thornfield Hall. There must be some mistake.'

Mr Rochester was silent for a long time. 'I can explain,' he said at last. 'I'll tell you everything. It is true. My wife is living at Thornfield Hall. We got married fifteen years ago in the West Indies, when I was a young man. My wife's name was Bertha Mason. She is Mason's sister. Soon after the wedding, Bertha became very strange. Slowly, she became **mad** and dangerous. She wanted to kill me, and she tried to kill anybody who came near her. Last April, she tried to kill her brother, Mr Mason.'

'Nobody knows about Bertha, nobody knows that she is my wife. This young lady, Jane Eyre, knows nothing about her. A nurse, Grace Poole, looks after Bertha.' Mr Rochester's face was dark and serious. 'Come with me,' he said, 'now I will take you all to see her.'

We all left the church. Without speaking, we returned to Thornfield Hall. When we got there, Mr Rochester took us

Someone threw open the doors at the back of the church, and shouted 'Stop the wedding!'

up to the attic. He took out a key and unlocked the door. Grace Poole was there, and in the room with her there was a frightening woman, the terrible woman that I saw in my bedroom, the person with the cruel, mad laugh! She was the person who tried to kill Mr Mason and who set fire to Mr Rochester's room! She was mad. But she was Mr Rochester's wife and I could not marry him.

Poor Mr Rochester! I felt sorry for him. But I could not now stay at Thornfield Hall.

'I must leave my home for ever,' I thought, with a heavy heart. 'I can never come back and I will never see Mr Rochester again.'

Sadly, I put a few ordinary clothes into a small bag. I did not take my beautiful new clothes. I took a little money and quietly left Thornfield Hall early one morning. I did not say goodbye to anybody and nobody saw me leave.

◆　　　◆　　　◆　　　◆

I wanted to travel as far away from Thornfield Hall as I could. I spent all my money. I travelled for two days and nights until at last I arrived at a place where there were no towns or villages and very few houses. I had no money now to buy food. I was very tired and very hungry.

It was evening and it was getting dark. I could see only one house. I went to the house and looked through the window. There were two young women in the room. They looked kind, so I knocked on the door. A servant opened it.

'Who are you?' she asked. 'What do you want?'

'I'm a stranger,' I said. 'I haven't any money or food. I'm tired and hungry. Please help me.'

The servant looked at me for a long time. 'I'll give you some bread,' she answered at last. 'But then you must go away.' She left me and came back with a piece of bread. 'Now go!' she said. 'You can't stay here.'

But I was too tired to move. I sat down on the ground by the door. 'Nobody will help me,' I said. 'I will die.'

I did not know, but someone was listening and watching me. 'You won't die,' he said.

I did not know, but someone was listening and watching me.

'You won't die,' he said. 'Who are you?' I looked up and saw a tall young man. He knocked loudly on the door. The servant opened it again.

'Hannah,' the man asked, 'who is this young woman?'

'I don't know,' said the servant, Hannah. 'I told her to go away, but she's still here. Go away!' she said to me.

'No, Hannah, she can't go away. She is ill and she needs our help. She must come inside,' the man said.

They took me into the house. The room was warm. The two young women came to talk to me.

'What's your name?' they asked.

'My name's Jane Elliot,' I said. I did not want anyone to know my real name. I did not want Mr Rochester to find me. I wanted to start again.

My new friends gave me some food and took me to a bedroom where I slept for a long time.

After a few days I felt better, and was able to talk to my kind new friends. Their names were Diana and Mary Rivers. The man was their brother. His name was St John Rivers and he was a clergyman. St John was a very handsome young man with fair hair and blue eyes. He was always very serious. He did not often laugh or smile. He was planning to go to India to work.

His sisters were more friendly but I did not want to tell them about Mr Rochester. I thanked them for their kindness. 'I have no family,' I said. 'My parents are both dead. I was at Lowood School for six years. After that, I got a job with a family, but I had to leave suddenly. I didn't do anything wrong. Please believe me.'

'Don't talk now,' said Diana. 'You are tired.'

'You will want a new job now,' said St John.

'Yes,' I replied. 'As soon as possible.'

'Good. I will help you.'

A month later, Diana and Mary left their home to work as teachers in the south of England. St John asked me to teach the children who lived near his church. They were poor children and the school was very small. I was the only teacher.

I enjoyed my work. I did not have much money and I had to work very hard. I lived in a very small house near the school. There were not many people there, but St John was very kind and gave me books to read. In my free time, I read and painted pictures. Sometimes, St John visited me in the evenings.

One evening, he came to my house when I was just finishing a painting. He looked at some of my pictures. Then he looked again, more closely, at one of the paintings. Without saying anything, he tore a piece of paper off the bottom of the painting, and put it carefully into his pocket. Then, quite suddenly, he left. I was very surprised. What a strange person he was!

The next day it snowed. I thought no visitors would come that day. But in the evening there was a knock on the door. It was St John. He was wet and cold.

'Why have you come? Is there bad news?' I asked. 'Are your sisters all right?'

'Don't worry. There is no bad news. Diana and Mary are both well,' he answered. He sat down in front of the fire. I waited but he said nothing. 'How strange he is!' I thought. 'Why did he come here when the weather is so bad? Perhaps he is bored. His sisters are far away.'

St John sat and thought for a long time. At last, he spoke.

'I know your story,' St John said. 'I know about your parents, and about Mrs Reed. I know about Lowood School. And I know about Thornfield Hall and about Mr Rochester. I also know about Mr Rochester's wife. So now I know why you came here without any money. I know why you left

Thornfield Hall. Mr Rochester must be a very bad man.'

'Oh, no. He isn't,' I said.

'I have had a letter,' said St John, 'from a man in London called Mr Briggs. He wants to find you. He asked about Jane Eyre. You call yourself Jane Elliot, but I know your real name is Jane Eyre. Look!' St John showed me a piece of paper. It was the piece of paper from the bottom of my painting. My real name, Jane Eyre, was on it.

'Did Mr Briggs say anything about Mr Rochester?' I asked. 'How is Mr Rochester?' I only wanted to know about Mr Rochester. I still loved him.

'Mr Briggs doesn't know anything about your Mr Rochester,' said St John. 'He wrote to me about your uncle, Mr Eyre of Madeira. Your uncle is dead. He has left you all his money. You are a very rich young woman.'

For a long time, I was too surprised to speak. I was rich now, but I was not excited. I tried to understand what it meant to be rich.

'I can't understand,' I said at last. 'Why did Mr Briggs write to you?'

'Because,' St John said, 'Mr Eyre of Madeira was also our uncle. He was my mother's brother. When he died, he left all his money to you, Jane Eyre.'

'Then you, Diana and Mary are my cousins!' I said. 'This is wonderful news! Our uncle's money is for all of us. Diana and Mary can come home, and we can all live together.' It was good to have money, but it was even better to have three cousins.

So, just before Christmas, Diana and Mary came home. I worked hard to make their old house comfortable. 'Diana and Mary will like it,' I thought. 'But what about St John? He's a strange man. He's like stone, hard and cold. He's pleased to see his sisters, but still he does not really look happy.'

Diana, Mary and I began to live quietly and comfortably together. St John still wanted to go to India. I was happy living with my cousins but I still thought about Mr Rochester every day. Where was he? Was he happy? I wrote to the **lawyer**, Mr Briggs, but Mr Briggs knew nothing about Mr Rochester. Then I wrote to Mrs Fairfax at Thornfield Hall. I waited for a letter from her, but no letter came. I wrote to Mrs Fairfax again; perhaps she did not get my first letter. Again there was no answer. At last, a letter did come for me, but it was only a letter from Mr Briggs about my uncle's money. I began to cry.

While I was crying, St John came into the room and saw me. 'Jane,' he said, 'come for a walk with me. No, don't call Diana and Mary. I want to talk to you.'

We walked along the side of the river. At first, St John said nothing. At last, he turned to me. 'Jane, I'm going to India in six weeks and I want you to come with me.'

I was surprised. Why did St John want me to go to India with him? How could I help him? I was not strong and serious like him.

'As your helper?' I asked. 'I don't think . . .'

'No, not as my helper. As my wife. I want to marry you, so that we can work together in India. There are many poor people there. They need our help.'

Now I was even more surprised. I felt sure that St John did not love me. And I did not want to marry him. I could not marry him. I still loved Mr Rochester.

'But I can't go to India,' I said. 'I don't know how to help the people there. I'm not like you.'

St John looked at me seriously. 'Oh, that doesn't matter. I'll tell you what to do and you'll quickly learn. You always worked hard in the village school. You'll work hard in India, too.'

I thought for a long time. St John, my cousin, needed my help. He was going to do very useful work in India. At last, I continued. 'Perhaps I can help you, but I must be free. I cannot marry you. You're like my brother,' I said.

I said 'Perhaps I can help you but I must be free. I cannot marry you.
You're like my brother.'

St John looked at me. His handsome face was cold and
serious, like stone. 'That's not possible. You must be my wife.
I don't want a sister. I don't want you to marry another man.
I want you to stay with me, to work with me, until we die.'

I felt cold and sad. I remembered my love for Mr Rochester
and the way he always spoke to me. St John was different. He
wanted me to marry him, but I knew he did not love me. I
wanted to help him, but not to marry him. He was a good
man, but I did not love him. I did not know what to say to him.

'I'm going away for two weeks,' St John continued. 'When
I come back, I want your answer. I hope you will decide to
marry me. You can't just stay here doing nothing.'

When I went back into the house, Diana spoke to me. 'Jane, you look unhappy. Your face is white. What is happening?'

I told her. 'St John asked me to marry him.'

'But that's wonderful!' she said. 'Now he will stay in England. He won't go to India. He'll stay here with us.'

'No,' I said, 'He wants me to go to India with him.'

'But you cannot go to India!' she said. 'You aren't strong enough.'

'I won't go,' I told her, 'because I can't marry St John. And now I'm afraid he's angry with me. He's a good man, but he doesn't understand how ordinary people feel.'

'I know,' Diana said. 'Our brother is a very good man, but he sometimes seems cold and hard.'

That night, I thought about St John for a long time. I did not know what to do. I did not love him, and he did not love me. But perhaps I could help him in India. I did not know what to do. The night was very quiet.

Suddenly, I thought I heard a voice. 'Jane! Jane! Jane!' it called. It was Mr Rochester's voice.

'Where are you?' I cried. But there was no answer. There was no one there. Was it only a dream? No, I knew that somewhere, far away, Mr Rochester needed me. 'I must go and find him,' I thought.

◆   ◆   ◆   ◆

The next day, I went to look for Mr Rochester. After a long journey, I arrived at Thornfield Hall. I walked for the last two miles to the house. I was excited; I was hurrying to see my old home again. The trees were the same, the road was the same. I arrived at the house and stopped . . . and stood and looked.

It was terrible! Where was Thornfield Hall, my beautiful home? No one could live here now. Now I understood why Mrs Fairfax never answered my letters. The walls of the house were still standing, but the windows were empty and dark and there was no roof. The grass was long and there

I arrived at the house and stopped . . . and stood and looked. It was terrible! No one could live here now.

were no flowers in the garden. The broken walls of the Hall were black and silent. The only sounds were the birds and the wind. Where was Mrs Fairfax now? Where was little Adèle? And where was Mr Rochester?

I hurried back to the village to find out. I asked a man in the village to tell me about Thornfield Hall.

'No one lives there now,' he told me. 'Last autumn, Thornfield Hall burned down. It was terrible. The house burned down in the middle of the night.'

'How did it happen?' I asked him.

'They think Mr Rochester's wife started it. Nobody ever saw her, but people say she was mad. People think she started a fire in her room in the attic. When it happened, the house was almost empty. Mr Rochester was in the house, but the little girl, Adèle, was away at school and old Mrs Fairfax was staying with some friends, many miles away. It seems that Mr Rochester did not want to see anybody at that time. People say he seemed very unhappy. They say that he wanted to marry a young woman, but she ran away.'

'Tell me about the fire,' I said.

'When the fire started,' he continued, 'Mr Rochester got all the servants out of the house, then he went back in to save his wife. She was still in the attic. But she climbed up on to the roof. I saw her there. She stood on the roof, shouting and waving her arms. Mr Rochester tried to help her, but he could do nothing. Suddenly, she fell from the roof.'

'Did she die?' I asked.

'Yes, she did. She died immediately, and Mr Rochester was very badly hurt. He could not get out of the burning house in time. When at last he came out, he was **blind**, and he had lost one hand.' The man shook his head.

So Mr Rochester was still alive! He was hurt, but he was not dead. Suddenly, I began to hope again. I continued to question the man.

'Where does Mr Rochester live now?' I asked. 'Does he live in England?'

'Yes,' the man answered. 'He cannot travel far, poor man. He lives at Ferndean, about thirty miles from here. It is a quiet place. He lives there quietly with two servants. He never has any visitors.'

I decided to go to Ferndean at once. I arrived there just before dark. As I got near the house, the front door opened and a man came out. I knew at once it was Mr Rochester. But he was very different now. He was still tall and strong, and his hair was still black. But his face looked sad, and he could not walk without help. At last, he turned and went sadly back into the house.

The servant, Mary, who answered the door, knew me at once. She was very surprised to see me. I told her that I knew all about Mr Rochester and the fire at Thornfield Hall. 'Tell Mr Rochester that he has a visitor. But don't tell him who it is.'

'He won't see you, Miss Jane,' she said. 'He won't see anybody now.'

I went into the room.

'Who's there?' Mr Rochester asked. 'Is that you, Mary? Answer me! What's happening?'

'Will you have some water?' I asked him.

'Who's that? Tell me!' he said. He was surprised and excited.

'Mary knows me,' I said. 'I only came this evening.' I took his hand.

'Jane? Is it Jane?' he asked. 'Jane, is it really you?'

'Yes, it is,' I said. 'I'm so happy to be with you again. I'll never leave you now.'

'But Jane, where did you go? What happened to you? Why did you leave Thornfield Hall so suddenly? Why did you go away without any money? Why did you not stay and let me help you?' he asked.

'You know why I left,' I said. 'I am sorry you were worried. But things are different now. I'm a rich woman,' I said. 'And I've got three cousins.' I told Mr Rochester all about my cousins and my new home.

'You do not need me now,' he said. 'But will you really stay with me?' There was hope in his voice again.

'Of course I will,' I said.

'But you're young. You'll want to get married some time. But not to me. I'm blind now and I can't do anything. You won't want to marry me. You'll want to marry some young man. What is your cousin, St John Rivers, like?' he asked. 'Is he an old man?'

'No. He is young and handsome.'

'Do you like him?' Mr Rochester asked.

'Yes, I do,' I answered. 'He's a very good man.'

'And does he like you?'

'Yes, I think so. He wants me to marry him.'

'And will you marry him?'

'No. I will not marry him. I do not love him.'

Mr Rochester looked suddenly happier. He took my hand. He was silent for a long time, and then he spoke. 'Jane, I can ask you again now: will you marry me?' he asked.

'Yes, I will,' I told him. At last, I felt really happy. And Mr Rochester, too, was no longer sad.

Three days later, I became Mr Rochester's wife.

I wrote to Diana and Mary. The news made them very happy. I also wrote to St John, but I had no answer from him. He went to India and continued to work very hard there. He never got married.

Mr Rochester and I are very happy together. We have been married for ten years now. Two years after we were married, Mr Rochester began to see again with one eye. He will never be able to see well, but he now can see me and he can see our children. Our story was a strange and sad one, and terrible things happened to us, but now at last we are happy together.

Then Mr Rochester spoke. 'Jane, I can ask you again now,' he said.
'Will you marry me?'

EXERCISES

Vocabulary Work

1 Look back at the 'Dictionary Words' in the story. Make lists of the words which are nouns, verbs and adjectives. One word can be a noun or a verb. Which is it?

2 Make sentences, using these pairs or groups of words:

a lawyer/to become/blind

b servant/attic

c servant/to pack

d clergyman/dream/mad

e cruel/lawyer/to tear

Comprehension

Pages 7–18

1 What are their names?

a Jane's aunt

b Jane's boy cousin

c Jane's best friend at school

d the head teacher

e Jane's student

f the man that Jane works for

2 Why did Mr Rochester's horse fall? What happened to him when he fell off his horse?

3 What did Jane:

a hear

b smell

c see

once at two o'clock in the morning? What did she do then?

Match the people and the places.

PEOPLE	PLACES
Mr Mason	Thornfield Hall
Jane's uncle, John Eyre	Lowood School
Helen Burns	the West Indies
Mrs Fairfax	Madeira

Who says these words? Who to?

a 'Come quickly! Help me!'

b 'Who lives in the attic?'

c 'What a night! Were you frightened?'

d 'I wrote to your uncle. I told him you were dead.'

e 'Stop the wedding! He has got a wife already!'

What was the name of the 'strange and frightening woman' who Jane saw on page 27? Who was she? What did she tear in pieces and why?

What was St John Rivers' job? What job did Jane get after she met the Rivers family?

What unpleasant surprise did Jane have when she went back to Thornfield Hall?

On page 41 Jane says: 'Things are different now.' What does she mean?

Discussion

Which of these people did Jane like? Which did she dislike? Why?

a	John Reed	f	Mr Brocklehurst
b	St John Rivers	g	Adèle
c	Helen Burns	h	Mrs Reed
d	Miss Temple	i	Diana Rivers
e	Mrs Fairfax	j	Blanche Ingram

Mr Rochester has a terrible family secret. Was he right to hide his wife in the attic? Why or why not?

You are making a film of the book *Jane Eyre*. Which film stars do you choose to play the people in the story? Why?

Writing

Write short descriptions of these people: Mr Rochester, St John Rivers, Blanche Ingram, John Reed, Bertha Mason (about 50 words each). Use some of these words:

proud	cold
handsome	mad
beautiful	frightening
rich	silent
poor	good
kind	interesting
cruel	unhappy

Review

Which part of the story was the most interesting? strange? frightening? sad? happy? Why?